SEASHORE & NAUTICAL

PATTERNS
for the Scroll Saw

by Wm. Hofferth

Fox
Chapel Publishing Co. Inc.
1970 Broad Street • East Petersburg, PA 17520 • www.foxchapelpublishing.com

Acknowledgments

For my Friend, Father and Biggest Fan:
William Joseph Hofferth
(January 26, 1937 – August 15, 2002)

Seashore and Nautical Patterns for the Scroll Saw is a brand new work, first published in 2003 by Fox Chapel Publishing Company, Inc. The patterns contained herein are copyrighted by the author. Artists purchasing this book may make any number of projects based on the patterns in this book for personal use, however mass
duplication for commercial purposes is strictly forbidden. The patterns themselves may be photocopied by the artist for his or her use in making the projects, but they are not to be duplicated for resale or distribution under any circumstances.

Publisher	Alan Giagnocavo
Book Editor	Ayleen Stellhorn
Desktop Specialist	Linda Eberly
Cover Design	Tim Mize

ISBN 1–56523–190–2
Library of Congress Preassigned Card Number: 2002117849

To order your copy of this book,
please send check or money order
plus $3.50 shipping to
Fox Books
1970 Broad Street
East Petersburg, PA 17520

Or visit us on the web at
www.foxchapelpublishing.com

Printed in China
10 9 8 7 6 5 4 3 2 1

Table of Contents

Introduction

DAVE OTFINOSKI

My family has been vacationing at the shore since I was very young. It was always an exciting time to be heading to the beach during the summer, and the sounds and the smells of the shore immediately invoke memories of those simple yet fun times at the beach. Now, in the middle of winter, my only connection to the shore is through the seaside décor found throughout our home. My scroll saw has enabled me to, in part, recreate some of the look and feel of the shore in my own home. Scrolling is relaxation for me, and if the projects that I produce and surround myself with can add to that relaxation, then I am doubly lucky.

I encourage you to "think outside of the box" when using these designs. In the gallery section of this book, I have illustrated how to use the designs to make silhouettes, clocks and other decorative pieces. However, with imagination they can be adapted to so many things. Use the star fish or shell designs as place cards at your next dinner gathering. Add an inlayed sea horse to the lid of a jewelry box for an added touch. Create a seasonal welcome sign and decorate it with differently painted lobsters: a red, white and blue one for summer, Easter colors for spring, fall foliage colors for autumn and Christmas colors for winter. Add accessories to silhouettes such as pens, names or business card holders. The possibilities are endless.

Enjoy!
Wm. Hofferth

Editor's note: You can see more of Bill's work at *www.willsworkshop.com* or e-mail him directly at *bill@willsworkshop.com*.

Helpful Hints

Getting Started
• Warm up by cutting the basic staircase design (Figure A) in a scrap piece of ¾" pine. This design requires you to use all of the skills needed to cut the designs in this book

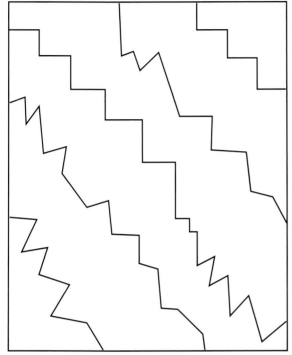

Figure A

• Keep a good coat of paste wax on the top surface of your table. This reduces the drag on your work piece.
• The patterns can be used at any size. Reduce or enlarge them to suit on a photocopier or computer.

Cutting
• Look and anticipate ahead of the blade. This allows you to regain the line if you start to stray off it.
   Never back up to get back on track! Gradually regain the line as you cut so that you don't interrupt the continuous cut of the blade.

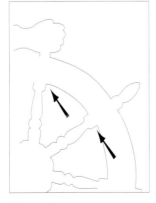

Figure B

• Start an inside cut on an inside corner (Figure B). This hides the point at which the cut began.
• Do not cut "off a pattern element" and continue (Figure C). This leaves a part of your project that is too sharp and that will chip and splinter later on. Try to exercise the moves from the staircase design to make the complete turn. This leaves a more finished or burnished edge less likely to chip or break later.

Figure C

Blades
• Use a #5 scroll saw blade for wood, and a #2 scroll saw blade for paper.

Material
• Do not cut material that is too thick or too thin. Finding the right thickness or stack of material is very important for success in scrolling. If the wood is too thick, you will be frustrated with blade breakage, burning of the material, and difficulty in getting through the project. If the wood is too thin, it presents another set of problems including not enough resistance to the blade, which makes it very difficult to turn and to stay on the lines.

Finishing
• If you are going to spray paint a piece, include a break-away tab into the design (Figure D). This gives you a place to hold the work while you paint. It is easily removed later with the score of a knife.
• Plan for the final display of your piece. An indoor display does not need any special finish, but a sign or weather vane will need special attention to withstand the elements.

Figure D

Castles in the Sand

Bayside Architect

Reading on the Beach

Summer Love

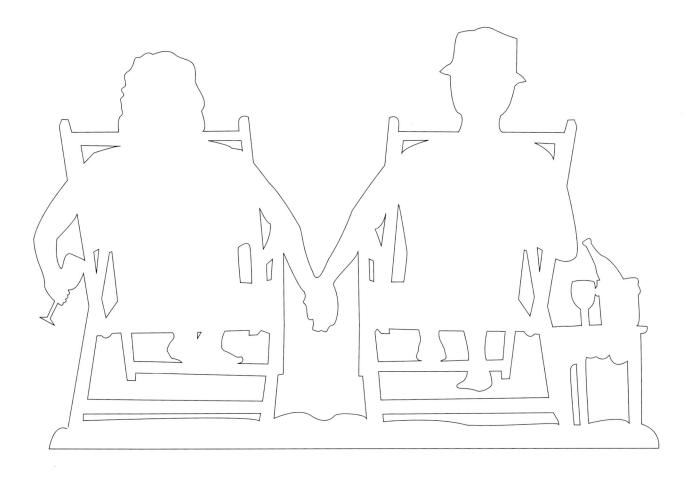

Seaside Stroll

Fishing Lesson

© Wm. Hofferth

Widow's Walk

Shore Bird

Sea Gull Look-Out

Sea Gull Signpost

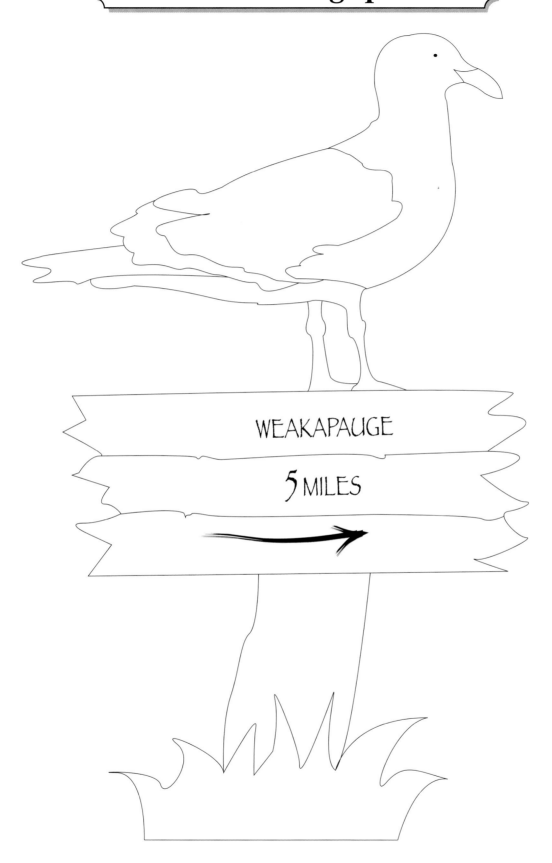

WEAKAPAUGE

5 MILES

Pelican

Piper Row

Flock of Gulls

Classic Lighthouse

Rocky Point–Lighthouse

Keeper of the Light

Lighthouse Ornament

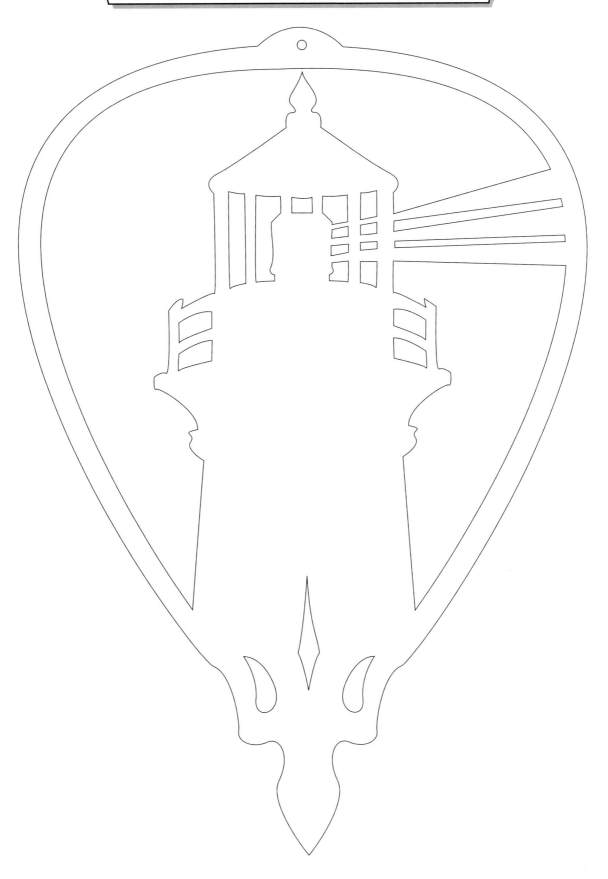

Lighthouse Mural

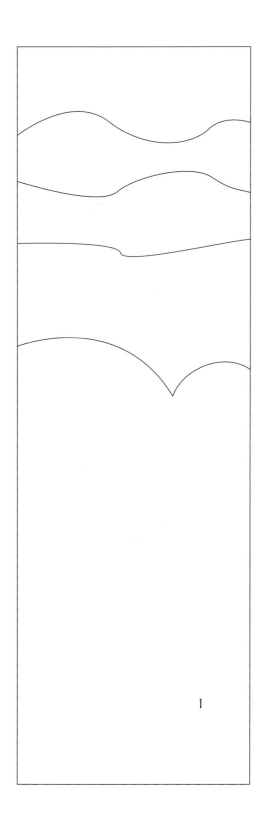

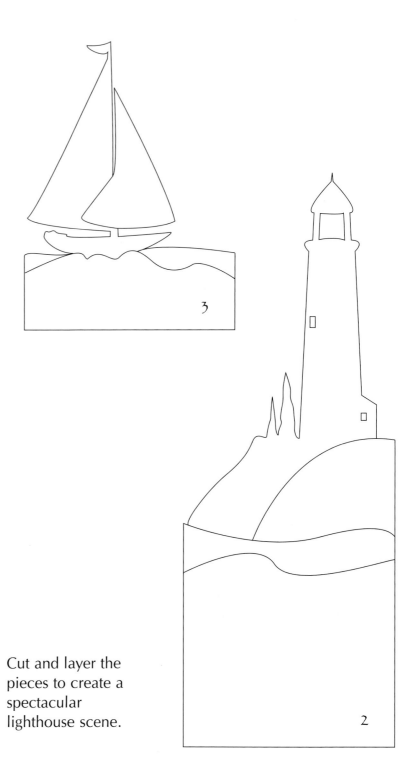

Cut and layer the
pieces to create a
spectacular
lighthouse scene.

© Wm. Hofferth

Sea Horse

Sea Horse II

Lobster

Crab

Sail Fish

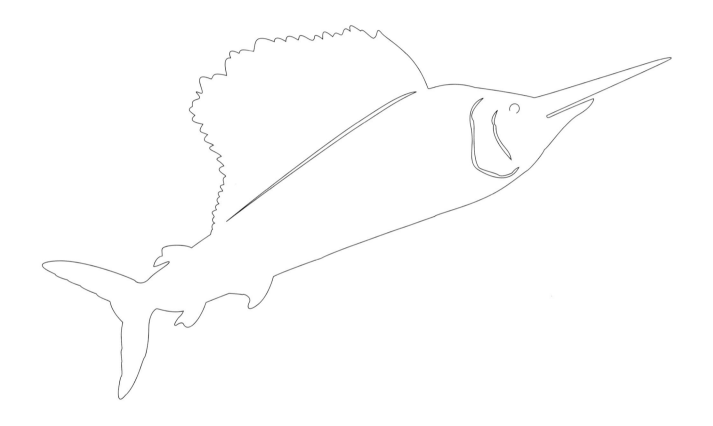

Sail Fish II

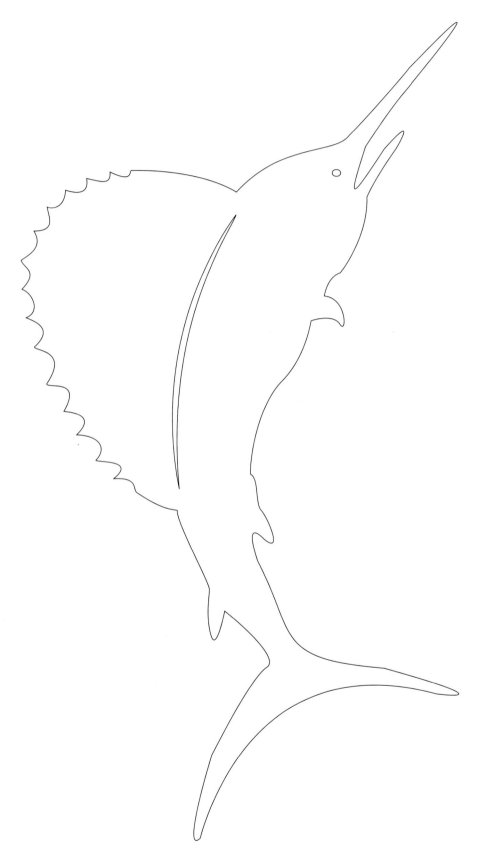

Fish

Dolphins

Whale Tail

Jaws

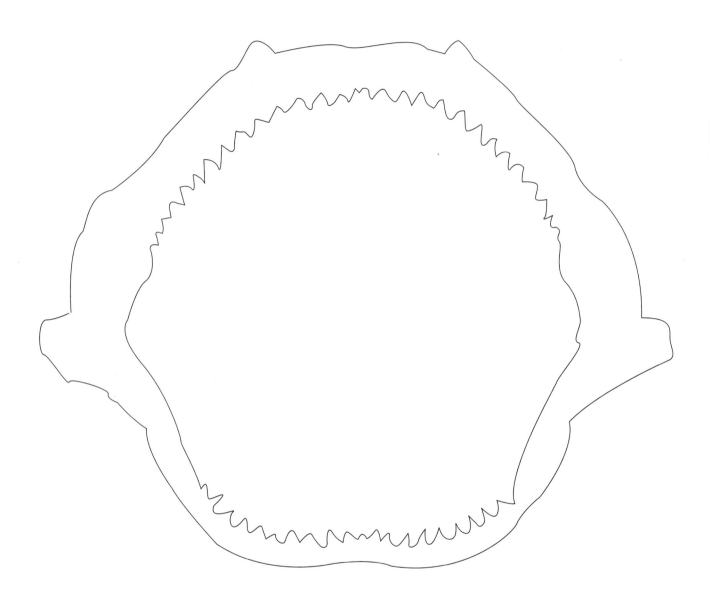

Sailor Beware – Lighthouse (pattern on page 16)

Sailor Clock (pattern on page 51)

Seahorse
  (pattern on page 21)

Seahorse II
  (pattern on page 22)

Sand Dollars (pattern on page 42)
Note: Sand dollars are cut from wood and
then dipped in Plaster of Paris.

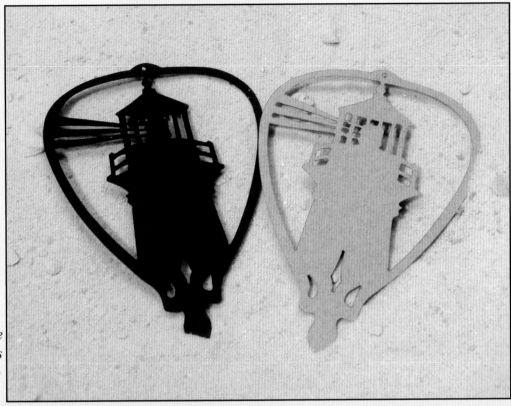

Lighthouse
Ornaments
(pattern on page 19)

Fox Chapel (anchor pattern on page 58)

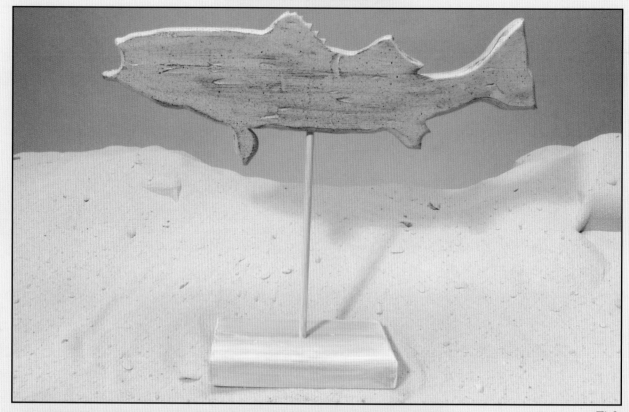

Fish
(pattern on page 27)

Lobster Shack
(pattern on page 64)

Lobster (pattern on page 23)

Sea Gull Look-Out (pattern on page 10)

Lighthouse Mural (pattern on page 20)

Sea Gull Signpost (pattern on page 11)

Bayside Architect (pattern on page 3)

Sand Dollar & Sea Shell

Sea Shells II

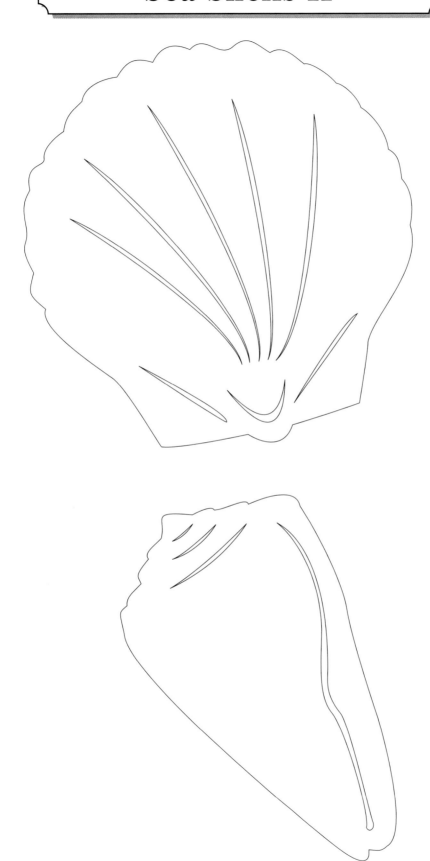

Nautilus

Starfish

Starfish II

Portrait of a Sea Captain

Mermaid Magic

Mermaid Ornament

© Wm. Hofferth

Ocean Sailor

Sailor Clock

SEASHORE & NAUTICA**L**
Patterns for the Scroll Saw

Tug Boat

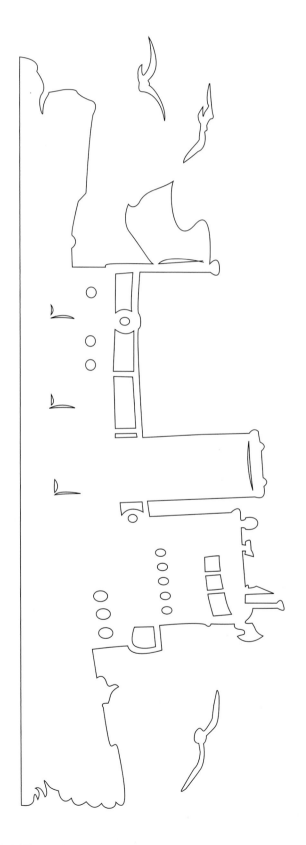

Ship in a Bottle

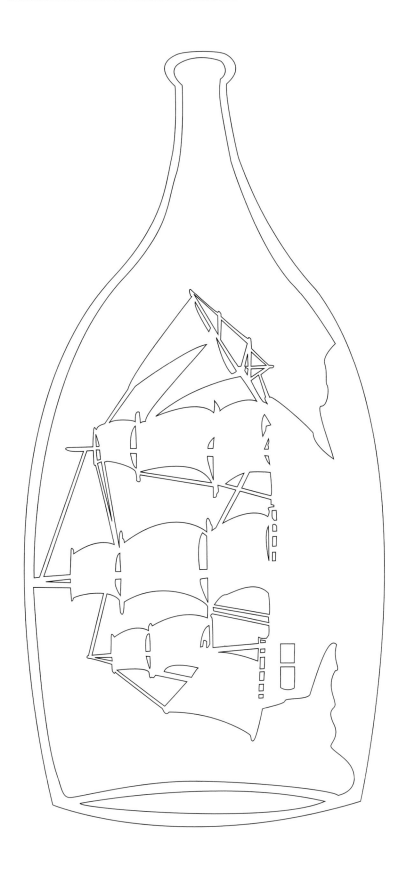

Ships Wheel Trivet

Oars & Preserver

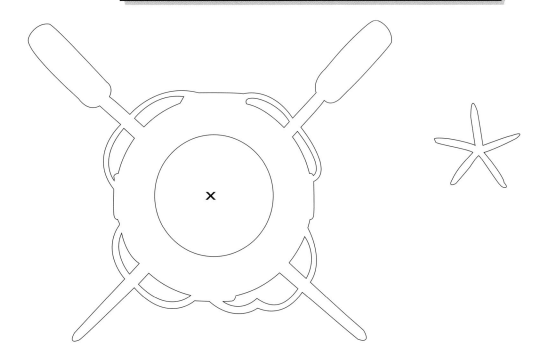

×

Add the oars and the preserver to this background piece to create a nautical thermometer, clock or barometer.

×

Anchors Away

Monster of the Deep

Pirate's Anchor

Ship Wreck

Deep Sea Diver

Wind Surfer

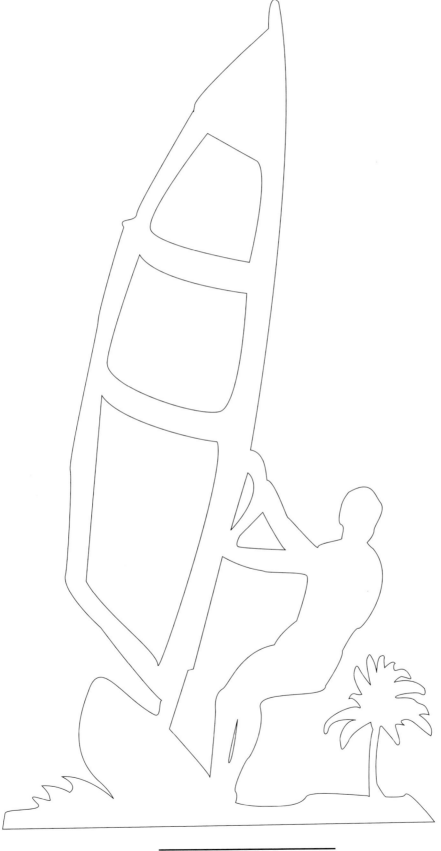

Wind Surfer II

Cut only the outline of this pattern. Use the interior lines as a guide to paint the cut pieces.

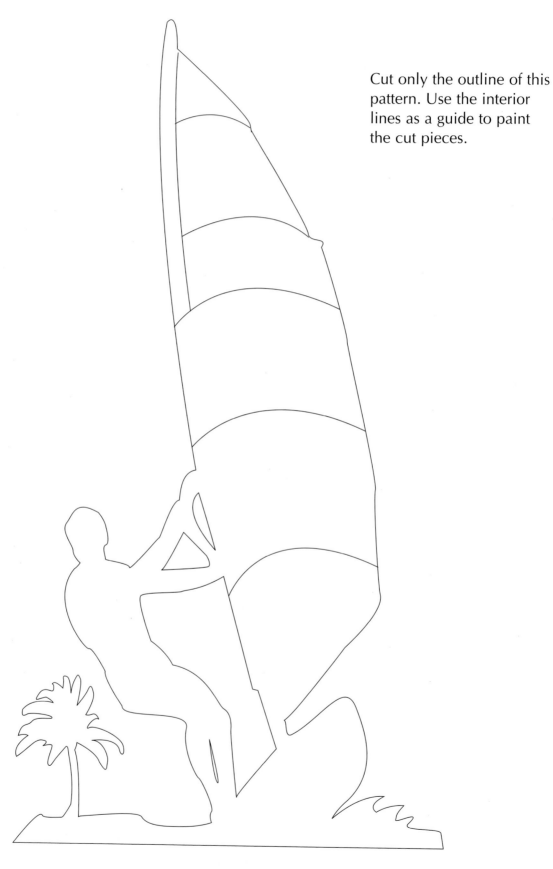

© Wm. Hofferth

© Wm. Hofferth

Lobster Shack

Lighthouse Weather Vane

Whale Weather Vane

Shovel & Pail

More Great Project Books from Fox Chapel Publishing